Book of Mormon
BRAIN
Bogglers

KEVAN J. KENNINGTON

CFI
An Imprint of Cedar Fort, Inc.
Springville, Utah

ISBN 13: 978-1-4621-1182-4

Published by CFI, an imprint of Cedar Fort, Inc.
2373 W. 700 S., Springville, UT 84663
Distributed by Cedar Fort, Inc., www.cedarfort.com

LIBRARY OF CONGRESS CATALOGING-IN-PUBLICATION DATA

Kennington, Kevan J., 1950– author.
Book of Mormon brain bogglers / Kevan J. Kennington.
    pages cm
Summary: Educational word puzzles, fill-in-the-blanks, matching activities, and other brain-busting "bogglers" that utilize information from the Book of Mormon.
ISBN 978-1-4621-1182-4
1. Book of Mormon. 2. Word games. I. Title.

BX8627.A2K47 2013
289.3'22--dc23

2012050716

Cover design by Shawnda Craig
Cover design © 2013 by Lyle Mortimer
Edited and typeset by Michelle Stoll

Printed in the United States of America

10 9 8 7 6 5 4 3 2 1

Contents

Number Bogglers

Within the pages of the Book of Mormon, you will find numbers of all kinds that are important—how long families traveled, how many people were involved, or how many spindles were in the Liahona. Your task is to match the correct numbers to the questions. I hope you enjoy the challenge!

Boggler #1

Book of Mormon Numbers, part 1

Your challenge in this section is to put the correct number in the blanks provided. *Answers page 76.*

2, 3, 4, 2, 8, 2, 600, 2, 5, 2, 1, 10's, 4, 1, 1000's, 50, 1, 30, 4, 50, 5, 600

1. (1 Nephi 1:4) Nephi lived in the ___ year of the reign of King Zedekiah.

2. (1 Nephi 2:6) Lehi traveled ___ days before pitching his tent.

3. (1 Nephi 3:31) Laban can command ___ men to slay us.

4. (1 Nephi 4:1) The Lord is mightier than Laban and his ___, yea, or even than his ___ of ___.

5. (1 Nephi 5:11) The brass plates contained the ___ book of Moses.

6. (1 Nephi 7:6) Ishmael had ___ daughters.

7. (1 Nephi 10:4) ___ years from the time that my father left Jerusalem, a prophet would the Lord God raise up.

8. (1 Nephi 14:10) Behold there are save ___ churches only.

9. (1 Nephi 16:10) And within the ball were ___ spindles.

10. (1 Nephi 7:6) There were ___ sons of Ishmael.

11. (1 Nephi 16:13) Lehi traveled ___ days, nearly in a south-southeast direction.

12. (1 Nephi 16:10) ___ spindle pointed the way whither we should go.

13. (1 Nephi 17:4) For ___ years did Lehi sojourn in the wilderness.

14. (1 Nephi 17:11) ___ stones did Nephi smite together to make fire.

15. (1 Nephi 18:7) Lehi begat ___ sons in the wilderness.

16. (1 Nephi 18:15) After ___ days of being driven back upon the sea, Nephi's brothers loosed his bands.

17. (1 Nephi 22:25) There shall be ___ fold and ___ shepherd.

18. (1 Nephi 22:25) The Lord shall gather his children from the ___ quarters of the earth.

19. (2 Nephi 5:28–30) ___ years after leaving Jerusalem, Nephi was commanded to make other plates.

Book of Mormon Numbers, part 2

3, 12, 600, 8, 3, 2, 2, 24, 1, 450, 9,
50, 30, 204, 16, 2, ½, 40, 24, 2, 43, 1

20. (2 Nephi 11:3) By the words of ___ the Lord will establish his words.

21. (2 Nephi 25:19–22) The Messiah to come ___ years from the time Lehi left Jerusalem.

22. (2 Nephi 27:12) ___ witnesses shall see the golden plates.

23. (2 Nephi 29:8) The testimony of ___ nations shall be a testimony unto us.

24. (2 Nephi 29:8) The Lord speaks the same words to ___ nation as he does another.

25. (Omni 1:21) Coriantumr lived with the people of Zarahemla for ___ moons.

26. (Mosiah 6:4) Mosiah began to reign in his ___ year.

27. (Mosiah 7:2) Mosiah granted ___ men to go up to the land of Lehi-Nephi to find their brethren.

28. (Mosiah 7:4) Ammon and his men wandered in the wilderness for ___ days.

29. (Mosiah 7:8) For ___ days Ammon and his companions were imprisoned by King Limhi's people.

30. (Mosiah 7:22) Limhi and his people paid ___ of all they had to the King of the Lamanites.

31. (Mosiah 8:7) Limhi sent ___ men to find the way back to Zarahemla.

32. (Mosiah 8:9) The search party found ___ gold plates while looking for the Lord of Zarahemla.

33. (Mosiah 12:1) For ___ years, Abinadi hid from King Noah.

34. (Mosiah 18:16) ___ souls followed Alma to the waters of Mormon to be baptized.

35. (Mosiah 18:18) ___ priest was ordained for every ___ people.

36. (Mosiah 18:35) ___ people followed Alma into the wilderness.

37. (Mosiah 20:5) King Noah's wicked priest captured ___ daughters of the Lamanites.

38. (Mosiah 22:16) The Lamanite army pursued Limhi and his people for ___ days.

39. (Mosiah 23:3) For ___ days, Alma and his people traveled in the wilderness to get away from the armies of King Noah.

40. (Mosiah 24:25) It took Alma and his people ___ days to find the land of Zarahemla.

Book of Mormon Numbers, part **3**

14, 3, 7, 2, 6, 1, 4, 82, 1, 2, 2,
63, 3500, 1, 1, 91, 9, 1 ½, 1, 0, 6, 1

41. (Mosiah 25:23) There were ___ churches in the land of Zarahemla.

42. (Mosiah 27:23) For the space of ___ days, Alma and the priest fasted and prayed for Alma the younger.

43. (Mosiah 27:34) Mosiah had ___ sons.

44. (Mosiah 29:45) Alma died when he was ___ years old.

45. (Mosiah 29:46) Mosiah died when he was ___ years old.

46. (Alma 4:5) In the seventh year of the reign of the judges, ___ people joined the church.

47. (Alma 1:1 and chapter heading) The first year of the judges began in ___ BC

48. (Alma 4:20) In the ___ year of the reign of the judges, Alma delivered the judgment seat up to Nephihah.

49. (Alma 11:25) Amulek was offered ___ onties to deny the living God.

50. (Alma 16:9–10) It took ___ day to destroy the city of Ammonihah, even though its citizens said God could not destroy it.

51. (Alma 17:4) Alma and the sons of Mosiah had been preaching the gospel for ___ years when they were reunited.

52. (Alma 17:26) Ammon had been serving King Lamoni for ___ days when Lamanites scattered the sheep at the water of Sebus.

53. (Alma 17:38) Ammon killed ___ men with the sling.

54. (Alma 17:38) Ammon slew ___ with the sword.

55. Alma 18:14) When Ammon asked the king what he could do for him, it took the king ___ hour(s) to respond.

56. (Alma 19:1–5) King Lamoni was thought to be dead for ___ days and ___ nights before the queen asked for Ammon's help.

57. (Alma 19:16) King Lamoni, his wife, his servants, and Ammon all fell to the earth while calling upon the spirit of the Lord, except for ___ Lamanite(s).

58. (Alma 19:22) ___ Lamanite(s) were struck dead when he/they tried to kill Ammon as he lay on the ground.

59. (Alma 22:32) It was ___ days' journey from the east sea to the west sea on the line Bountiful and the land of Desolation.

60. (Alma 23:14) Many Lamanites were converted in Alma 23, along with _____ Amalekites and _____ Amulonites.

Boggler #2

The Book of Mormon Comes Forth

Listed below you will find significant dates and events with regard to the coming forth of the Book of Mormon. Can you match them correctly?

Answers page 76.

July **1828**, AD **421**, November **1829**, June **1828**, August **1829**, February **1828**, September **1823**, April **1829**, August **1829**, June **1829**, September **1827**

_____ 1. Moroni buries the gold plates.

_____ 2. Joseph Smith first sees the gold plates.

_____ 3. Joseph Smith obtains the plates.

_____ 4. Gold plates are taken from Joseph Smith because Martin Harris lost some manuscript pages.

_____ 5. Oliver Cowdery comes to Joseph Smith's home.

_____ 6. A second manuscript of the Book of Mormon is prepared.

_____ 7. E. B. Grandin agrees to print the Book of Mormon.

_____ 8. The translation of the Book of Mormon is completed.

_____ 9. Martin Harris takes manuscript to Charles Anthon.

_____ 10. Martin Harris loses the first 116 pages of the manuscript.

_____ 11. Martin Harris mortgages his farm to pay for the printing of the Book of Mormon.

Boggler #3

Book of Mormon Birthdays

C an you match the individuals listed below with their approximate birth years? The scripture references listed after each name will help you estimate each answer.

Answers page 77.

A. 126 BC

B. 592 BC

C. 390 BC

D. 615 BC

E. AD 311

F. 2200 BC

G. 190 BC

H. 515 BC

I. 54 BC

J. AD 360

K. 30 BC

L. 174 BC

_____ 1. King Benjamin (Omni 1:23)

_____ 2. Nephi, son of Helaman (Helaman 2:2)

_____ 3. Nephi, one of the twelve disciples (3 Nephi 1:1)

_____ 4. Enos (Jacob 7:27)

_____ 5. Alma the Younger (Mosiah 29:47)

_____ 6. Omni (Omni 1:1)

_____ 7. Nephi, son of Lehi (1 Nephi 1:4)

_____ 8. Brother of Jared (Ether 1:33)

_____ 9. Mormon (Mormon 1:2)

_____ 10. Alma the Elder (Mosiah 17:2)

_____ 11. Jacob (1 Nephi 18:7)

_____ 12. Moroni, Mormon's son (Mormon 1:8)

Boggler #4

Pages, Pages, How Many Pages?

C an you match the number of pages to the corresponding book?

Answers page 77.

Note: There are two books with 18.5 pages, so "A" will be the answer to TWO questions.

Number of pages	Books
A. 18.5	_____ 1. 1 Nephi
B. 38	_____ 2. 2 Nephi
C. 31	_____ 3. Jacob
D. 161	_____ 4. Enos
E. 52.5	_____ 5. Jarom
F. 58	_____ 6. Omni
G. 2	_____ 7. Mosiah
H. 4	_____ 8. Alma
I. 64	_____ 9. Helaman
J. 13.5	_____ 10. 3 Nephi
K. 62	_____ 11. 4 Nephi
L. 2.5	_____ 12. Mormon
M. 3	_____ 13. Ether
	_____ 14. Moroni

Boggler #5

Time in a Book

Can you match the number of years a book covered (approximately) to the corresponding book?

Answers page 77.

Number of years	Books
A. 63	_____ 1. 1 Nephi
B. 40	_____ 2. 2 Nephi
C. 286	_____ 3. Jacob
D. 39	_____ 4. Enos
E. 62	_____ 5. Jarom
F. 21	_____ 6. Omni
G. 35	_____ 7. Mosiah
H. 13	_____ 8. Alma
I. 79	_____ 9. Helaman
J. 59	_____ 10. 3 Nephi
K. 43	_____ 11. 4 Nephi
L. 52	_____ 12. Mormon
M. 230	_____ 13. Moroni

Matching Bogglers

W ho is who, what is what, and where is that? The people and objects in these next bogglers are easy to get mixed up. Match the items with their correct characteristics or scripture. It's up to you to make the connections!

Boggler #6

Alma Who?

Can you match the correct Alma to his unique features? *Answers page 77.*

A. Alma the Younger
B. Alma the Elder

_____ 1. Wrote the words of Abinadi.

_____ 2. Was presiding high priest and chief judge.

_____ 3. Guided 450 souls into the wilderness.

_____ 4. Organized the church in the land of Zarahemla.

_____ 5. Associate of the sons of the king.

_____ 6. Was an associate of Amulon.

_____ 7. Pleaded for a prophet's life to be spared.

_____ 8. Slew Amlici, who wanted to be king.

_____ 9. An angel asked, "Why persecutest thou the Church of God?"

_____ 10. "His death or burial" remains a mystery.

_____ 11. Suffered the pains of hell for three days and three nights.

_____ 12. Built a city in the land of Helam.

Boggler #7

Scripture Plates

The Book of Mormon is compiled from a number of scriptural plates. Listed below are some of the plates and their features. Can you match each set of plates with their unique feature?
Answers page 77.

A. Brass plates

B. Small plates of Nephi

C. Large plates of Nephi

D. 24 gold plates

E. Plates of Mormon

____ 1. The Spirit inspired Mormon to add them to the plates.

____ 2. Contained prophesies of Joseph of old.

____ 3. Contained the book of Lehi.

____ 4. Translated by Mosiah first.

____ 5. Written in Egyptian.

____ 6. Moroni added to these plates.

____ 7. Second set of plates that Nephi wrote.

____ 8. Contains the abridgement of the large plates of Nephi.

____ 9. Contained a "full account of the history" of the Nephites.

____ 10. Found by an expedition sent out by King Limhi.

____ 11. Contained "the more sacred things."

Boggler #8

Keepers of the Records

Listed below are a number of individuals who were keepers of the sacred records. Can you place them in the correct chronological order?

Answers page 77.

Enos, Abinadom, Nephi, Shiblon, Benjamin, Alma the Younger, Amaleki, Jarom, Mosiah (son of Mosiah), Amaron, Jacob, Chemish, Lehi, Helaman (son of Helaman), Omni

1._____   2._____
3._____   4._____
5._____   6._____
7._____   8._____
9._____   10._____
11._____   12._____
13._____   14._____
15._____

Boggler #9

Family Business

F our Nephite families kept the plates—namely Lehi, Alma, Mosiah, and Mormon's posterities. Can you identify who belongs to which family?

Answers page 78.

A. Lehi's family

B. Mosiah's family

C. Alma's family

D. Mormon's family

____ 1. Amos, son of Nephi

____ 2. Mosiah

____ 3. Moroni

____ 4. Shiblon

____ 5. Nephi, son of Helaman

____ 6. Enos

____ 7. Amaron

____ 8. Benjamin

____ 9. Nephi, son of Lehi

____ 10. Ammaron

____ 11. Omni

Boggler #10

Kings in the Book of Mormon

C an you match the kings with their unique experiences, characteristics, or relationships? Answers can be used more than once. *Answers page 78.*

A. Mosiah I

B. Benjamin

C. Mosiah II

D. Zeniff

E. Noah

F. Limhi

G. Lamoni

___ 1. Became king when his father was killed.

___ 2. Grandfather of Limhi.

___ 3. Was warned to leave the land of Nephi.

___4. Heavy taxer of his people.

___5. His father sought to slay him.

___6. Left Zarahemla for ancestral land.

___7. Proposed judges instead of kings.

___8. Had a tower built so he could preach to his people.

___9. Gideon helped this king escape.

___ 10. Thought Ammon was the Great Spirit.

___11. Amaleki gave him the records.

___ 12. Translated writing that was on a stone.

___13. Suffered death by fire.

___ 14. Translated Jaredite records.

Boggler #11

Roaming in the Wilderness

Much has been learned abut Lehi and his family during their trek through the wilderness. Can you match the people with their unique features?
Answers page 78.

A. Joseph

B. Jacob

C. Zedekiah

D. Lehi

E. Laban

F. Zoram

G. Moses

H. Laman

I. Lemuel

J. Sam

K. Ishmael

L. Sariah

____ 1. Had a fine sword.

____ 2. Firstborn in the days of his father's tribulations.

____ 3. A valley was named for him.

____ 4. His writings were on the brass plates.

____ 5. Died while roaming in the wilderness.

____ 6. Last-born in the wilderness.

____ 7. The third son of Lehi.

____ 8. A descendant of Judah.

____ 9. In Lehi's dream, partook of the fruit along with Nephi and Sam.

____ 10. A river was named for him.

____ 11. Saw a pillar of light.

____ 12. Had the key to Laban's treasury.

Boggler #12

Doctrinal Message Search

Many of the chapters in the Book of Mormon discuss specific topics. Can you match the messages with their chapters?
Answers page 78.

A. Repentance and baptism   ____ 1. 1 Nephi 1

B. Prophecies of Christ   ____ 2. 1 Nephi 8

C. Belief in Christ   ____ 3. 1 Nephi 11

D. Prayer   ____ 4. 1 Nephi 19

E. Calling of a prophet   ____ 5. 2 Nephi 2

F. Chastity and consecration   ____ 6. 2 Nephi 4

G. Condescension of God   ____ 7. 2 Nephi 9

H. Salvation and Atonement   ____ 8. 2 Nephi 25

I. The Holy Ghost   ____ 9. 2 Nephi 28

J. Opposition and choice   ____ 10. 2 Nephi 30

K. The ways of Satan   ____ 11. 2 Nephi 31

L. Psalm of Nephi   ____ 12. 2 Nephi 32

M. Millennial era   ____ 13. Jacob 2

N. Lehi's dream   ____ 14. Jacob 5

O. Allegory of the olive tree   ____ 15. Enos

Boggler #13

Doctrinal Message Search, part 2

Many of the chapters in the Book of Mormon discuss specific topics. Can you match the chapters with their messages? *Answers page 78.*

A. Mosiah 2

B. Mosiah 3

C. Mosiah 4

D. Mosiah 5

E. Mosiah 14

F. Mosiah 18

G. Mosiah 27

H. Mosiah 29

I. Alma 5

J. Alma 7

K. Alma 12

L. Alma 13

M. Alma 17

N. Alma 32

O. Alma 34

____1. Covenant-making children of Christ

____2. Good government

____3. The suffering Messiah/Isaiah 53

____4. The Atonement; the Savior is born of Mary

____5. First and second death

____6. Serving and thanking God

____7. Faith

____8. Missionary work

____9. The Atonement and the natural man

____10. Priesthood

____11. Conversion of Alma

____12. Giving to the poor

____13. Procrastination/Atonement

____14. Remaining born again

____15. The covenant of baptism

Boggler #14

Doctrinal Message Search, part 3

Many of the chapters in the Book of Mormon discuss specific topics. Can you match the chapters with their messages? *Answers page 78.*

A. Preaching with great power/righteousness

B. Prophecies of the signs of Christ's birth

C. Christ's spirit body

D. Be careful how you judge others

E. Christ's initial appearance

F. The Church and gospel of Jesus Christ

G. Resurrection

H. The sacrament

I. Salvation of children

J. The new law of Christ

K. Faith, hope, and charity

L. Counsel with the Lord

M. The unstableness of man

N. Blessing the sick; children and parents

O. Justice and mercy

____ 1. Alma 37

____ 2. Alma 40

____ 3. Alma 42

____ 4. Helaman 5

____ 5. Helaman 12

____ 6. Helaman 14

____ 7. 3 Nephi 11

____ 8. 3 Nephi 12

____ 9. 3 Nephi 14

____ 10. 3 Nephi 17

____ 11. 3 Nephi 18

____ 12. 3 Nephi 27

____ 13. Ether 3

____ 14. Moroni 7

____ 15. Moroni 8

Boggler #15

Disbelievers of the Book of Mormon

C an you match the disbelievers with the statements listed below that relate to them? *Answers page 79.*

    A. Korihor (Alma 30)   C. Sherem (Jacob 7)

    B. Nehor (Alma 1)   D. Zeezrom (Alma 11)

_____ 1. Taught that all mankind should be saved

_____ 2. He and others did stir up the people to rioting and all manner of disturbance

_____ 3. Came forth in the first year of the reign of the judges

_____ 4. The people of Ammon at Jershon would not listen to him

_____ 5. Said that the people were not keeping the law of Moses

_____ 6. Offered Amulek six onties of silver if he would deny the existence of a supreme being

_____ 7. Introduces priestcraft among the people

_____ 8. Confessed that the devil had deceived him and had appeared unto him in the form of an angel

_____ 9. Was baptized and became a missionary

_____ 10. Was told if the curse was removed from him, he would try to lead the people astray again

_____ 11. Taught that priests and teachers should be popular

_____ 12. He was trampled to death by the people he had led astray

_____ 13. Asked for a sign by the Holy Ghost

_____ 14. Asked that the people be called together so he could speak to them before he died

_____ 15. A lawyer living in Ammonihah

_____ 16. The power of the Lord came upon him, and he fell to the earth

Boggler #16

Disbelievers—Who Said That?

C an you match the disbelievers with their message and questions? *Answers page 79.*

> A. Korihor (Alma 30)   C. Sherem (Jacob 7)
>
> B. Nehor (Alma 1)   D. Zeezrom (Alma 11)

_____ 1. "O ye that are bound down under a foolish and a vain hope, why do you yoke yourselves with such foolish things?"

_____ 2. "Is there more than one God? Who is he that shall come? Is it the Son of God?"

_____ 3. "Priest and teachers ought not to labor with their hands, but that they ought to be supported by the people."

_____ 4. "Brother Jacob I have sought much opportunity that I might speak unto you; . . . ye have led away much of this people that they pervert the right way of God."

_____ 5. "I fear lest I have committed the unpardonable sin."

_____ 6. "All mankind should be saved at the last day, and that they need not fear nor tremble."

_____ 7. "Shall he save his people in their sins?"

_____ 8. "Ye look forward and say that ye see a remission of your sins. But behold, it is the effect of a frenzied mind."

Complete the Scriptural Phrases Bogglers

This section includes important phrases from the scriptures, but several words are missing. Your challenge is to fill in the blanks to make the scriptures complete!

Boggler #17

The Devil Made Me Do It!

In 2 Nephi 28, the teachings of the devil and his followers in these latter days are described. Listed below, you will find some of these teachings with key words missing. Can you correctly match the key words with the corresponding teaching of the devil?
Answers page 79.

puffed, advantage, work, learning, pit, power, hide,
high, little, rob, no, stiff, merry, miracles, deny, die

1. "Eat, drink and be _____, for tomorrow we _____."

2. "Yea, lie a _____, take the _____ of one because of his words."

3. "Dig a _____ for thy neighbor."

4. "For this day he is not a God of _____; he hath done his _____."

5. "And hear ye our precept; for behold there is _____ God today."

6. "And they deny the _____ of God."

7. "They shall teach with their _____ and _____ the Holy Ghost."

8. "Many . . . shall be _____ up in their hearts, and shall seek deep to _____ their counsels from the Lord."

9. "They _____ the poor because of their fine sanctuaries."

10. "They wear _____ necks and _____ heads."

Boggler #18

The Faith Experiment.

In Alma 32, Alma gives a great discourse on faith. Listed below are some of Alma's teachings with key words missing. Can you match the correct words with its scriptural phrase? *Answers page 79.*

hope, compelled, swell, cause, arouse, seed, heart, everlasting, knoweth, experiment, cast, likeness, root, not, perfect, forward, nourishment, root, cursed, particle, true, faith

1. "Now I ask, is this faith? . . . Nay: for if a man knoweth a thing he hath no _____ to believe, for he _____ it."

2. "Faith is not to have a _____ knowledge of things."

3. "Therefore if ye have faith ye _____ for things which are _____ seen, which are true."

4. "How much more _____ is he that knoweth the will of God and doeth it not."

5. "Blessed are they who humble themselves without being _____ to be humble."

6. "If ye will awake and _____ your faculties, even to an _____ upon my words, and exercise a _____ of faith."

7. "Now, we will compare the word unto a _____."

8. "If ye give place, that a seed may be planted in your _____, behold if it be a _____ seed, or a good seed, if ye do not _____ it out by your unbelief, that ye will resist the Spirit of the Lord, behold, it will begin to _____ within your breast."

9. "For every seed bringeth forth unto its own _____."

10. "But if ye neglect the tree, and take no thought for its _____, behold it will not get any _____."

11. "But if you nourish the word, . . . by your _____ with great diligence, and with patience looking _____ to the fruit thereof, it shall take _____; and behold it shall be a tree springing up unto _____ life."

Boggler #19

Procrastinate? I'll Do That Tomorrow!

In Alma 34, Amulek sets forth profound teachings on the Atonement and procrastination. Listed below are some of those teachings with key words missing. Can you restore the key words to Amulek's messages? *Answers page 79.*

justice, eternal, last, Son, man, infinite, world, perish, faith, exposed, pointing, procrastinated, God, sacrifice, mercy, mercy, short, prepare, meet, human, sacrifice, repentance, mankind, atone, life, fowl, death, overpowereth, suffice

1. "There must be an atonement made, or else all _____ must unavoidably _____."

2. "For it is expedient that there should be a great and _____ sacrifice; yea not a sacrifice of _____, neither of beast, neither of any manner of _____; for it shall not be a _____ sacrifice; but, it must be an _____ and _____ sacrifice."

3. "Now there is not any man that can _____ his own blood which will _____ for the sins of another."

4. "There can be nothing which is _____ of an infinite atonement which will _____ for the sins of the _____."

5. "This is the whole meaning of the law, every whit _____ to that great and last sacrifice; and that great and last sacrifice will be the _____ of _____, yea, infinite and eternal."

6. "This being the intent of this last _____, to bring about the bowels of _____, which _____ justice, and bringeth about means unto man that they may have faith unto _____."

7. "And thus _____ can satisfy the demands of _____."

8. "He that exercises no _____ unto repentance is _____ to the whole law of the demands of justice."

9. "This _____ is the time for men to _____ to _____ God."

10. "If ye have _____ the day of your repentance until _____, behold, ye have become subjected to the spirit of the devil, he doth seal you his."

Boggler #20

Opposition Needed?

2 Nephi 2 is a discourse from Lehi to his son Jacob, wherein he teaches the need for opposition, the Fall, and agency. Listed below are some of his teachings with key words missing. Can you restore the key words to their proper places?
Answers page 79.

joy, remained, same, children, good, knowing, bitter, forever, sin, tree, die, driven, created, innocence, forbidden, evil, partaken, free, miserable, must, act, choose

1. "For it _____ needs be, that there is an opposition in all things."

2. "There was an opposition; even the _____ fruit in opposition to the _____ of life; the one being sweet and the other _____."

3. "Wherefore, the Lord God gave unto man that he should _____ for himself."

4. "He (the devil) said, Partake of the forbidden fruit, and ye shall not _____, but ye shall be as God, _____ good from _____."

5. "And after Adam and Eve had _____ of the forbidden fruit they were _____ out of the garden of Eden, to till the earth."

6. "If Adam had not transgressed he would have _____ in the garden of Eden. And all things which were _____ must have remained in the _____ state in which they were after they were created; and they must have remained _____, and had no end."

7. "And they would have had no _____; wherefore they would have remained in a state of _____, having no _____, for they knew no misery; doing no _____, for they know no _____."

8. "Men are _____ according to the flesh."

9. "They (men) are free to _____ liberty and eternal life."

10. "For he (Satan) seeketh that all men might be _____ like unto himself."

Boggler #21

Tell Me What Will Happen.

Alma 40 is a wonderful discourse on the resurrection, which Alma delivers to his son Corianton. Can you match the key words that have been left out of this lesson taught by a father to his son? *Answers page 80.*

time, good, troubles, forth, remain, darkness, chose, rest, righteous, all, reuniting, fiery, part, paradise, happiness, time, body, lost, joint, hair, soul, restored

1. "There is a time that _____ shall come _____ from the dead."

2. "There is a space of _____ between the time of death and the resurrection"

3. "The spirits of those who are _____ are received into a state of _____, which is called _____, a state of rest, a state of peace, where they shall _____ from all their _____ and from all care, and sorrow."

4. "The spirits of the wicked, yea, who are evil—for behold, they have no _____ nor portion of the spirit of the Lord; for behold, they _____ evil works rather than _____."

5. "Now this is the state of the souls of the wicked, yea, in _____, and a state of awful, fearful looking for the _____ indignation of the wrath of God upon them; thus they _____ in this state, as well as the righteous in paradise, until the _____ of their resurrection."

6. "It (resurrection) meaneth the _____ of the soul with the body."

7. "The soul shall be restored to the _____, and the body to the _____: . . . every limb and _____ shall be _____ to its body ... even a _____ of the head shall not be _____."

Boggler #22

Mercy, Mercy Appeasing Justice.

In Alma 42, Alma the Younger teaches his son Corianton about justice and mercy. Some of these teachings are listed below, but key words have been left out. Can you restore the correct words to complete Alma's teachings to his son?
Answers page 80.

> just, penitent, her, saved, none, demands, reclaimed, means, temporally, will, redemption, cease, grasp, spiritually, destroy, mankind, disobedience, repentance, spiritual, mercy, atoneth, merciful, resurrection, appease, atonement, destroyed

1. "Our first parents were cut off both _____ and _____ from the presence of the Lord; and thus we see they became subject to follow after their own _____."

2. "They (mankind) were cut off from the presence of the Lord, it was expedient that mankind should be _____ from this _____ death."

3. "There was no _____ to reclaim men from this fallen state, which man had brought upon himself because of his own _____."

4. "According to justice the plan of _____ could not be brought about, only on condition of _____."

5. "Mercy could not take effect except it should _____ the work of justice. Now the work of justice could not be _____; if so, God would _____ to be God."

6. "And thus we see that all _____ were fallen, and they were in the _____ of justice."

7. "The plan of _____ could not be brought about except an _____ should be made; therefore God himself _____ for the sins of the world, to bring about the plan of mercy, to _____ the demands of

justice, that God might be a perfect, _____ God, and a ___ God also."

8. "Mercy claimeth the _____."

9. "The atonement bringeth to pass the_____ of the dead."

10. "Justice exerciseth all his _____ and also mercy claimeth all which is _____ own; and thus, _____ but the truly penitent are _____."

Restoring Bogglers

These puzzles are full of names of important people in the scriptures. Either the vowels or the consonants will be missing. Can you figure out who it is?

Boggler #23

Restoring the Vowels

Restore the correct vowels in the blanks provided to discover a name in the Book of Mormon. *Answers page 80.*

Example: __ d __ m = Adam

1. M __ s __ s
2. L __ c h __ n __ __ s
3. N __ p h __ h __ h
4. N __ h __ r
5. M __ r __ n __
6. H __ l __ r __ m
7. J __ r __ m
8. L __ h __
9. G __ d d __ n __ h
10. __ b __ n __ d __
11. __ m l __ c __
12. G __ d __ __ n t __ n
13. __ __ r __ n
14. K __ m __ n
15. __ m m __ n
16. M __ r m __ n
17. N __ __ m
18. M __ s __ __ h
19. J __ n __ s

Boggler #24

Restoring Vowels, part 2

Restore the correct vowels in the blanks provided to discover a name in the Book of Mormon. *Answers page 80.*

1. H __ l __ m __ n
2. __ m __ s
3. L __ m __ n __
4. C __ __ z __ r __ m
5. G __ d g __ d d __ n __
6. J __ s __ p h
7. __ m __ l __ n
8. H __ g __ t h
9. K __ s h k __ m __ n
10. __ n t __ p __ s
11. C __ m
12. __ d __ m
13. B __ n j __ m __ n
14. H __ l __ m
15. L __ m __ n
16. __ b __ s h
17. G __ d __ __ __ n
18. K __ s h
19. __ m __ l __ k
20. C h __ m __ s h

Boggler #25

Restoring the Vowels, part 3

Restore the correct vowels in the blanks provided to discover a name in the Book of Mormon. *Answers page 80.*

1. C __ r __ __ n t __ m r
2. H __ m
3. J __ c __ b
4. __ l m __
5. M __ l __ k
6. __ t h __ r
7. M __ r __ __ n t __ n
8. __ m __ r __ n
9. L __ m __ __ l
10. H __ m n __
11. L __ b __ n
12. __ v __
13. L __ m h __
14. H __ l __ m
15. __ m __ l __ c k __ __ h
16. __ n __ s
17. __ s h m __ __ l
18. J __ r __ d
19. K __ r __ h __ r
20. C __ r __ __ n t __ m

35

Boggler #26

Restoring the Vowels, part 4

R estore the correct vowels in the blanks provided to discover a name in the Book of Mormon. *Answers page 81.*

1. __ m n __ r
2. P __ c __ m __ n __
3. S h __ r __ m
4. P __ h __ r __ n
5. S __ r __ h
6. Z __ n __ f f
7. S __ __ z __ r __ m
8. P __ c h __ s
9. S h __ b l __ m
10. S __ m __ __ l
11. S h __ m n __ n
12. Z __ __ z r __ m
13. P __ __ n c h __
14. S __ t h
15. S __ m
16. N __ m r __ d
17. Z __ d __ k __ __ h
18. S __ r __ __ h
19. N __ __ h
20. P __ g __ g

Boggler #27

Restoring the Consonants

R estore the correct consonants in the blanks provided and discover a name from the Book of Mormon. *Answers page 81.*

Example: A _ a _ = Adam

1. __ a __
2. A a __ o __
3. A __ a __ o __
4. A __ a __ e __ i
5. __ a __ e __
6. A __ i __ __
7. A __ i __ a __ i
8. __ a __ i a __ __ o __
9. A __ __ o __
10. A __ o __
11. __ a __ o __ __
12. A __ u __ e __
13. A __ u __ o __
14. __ a __ u e __
15. __ e __ a __
16. __ e a __ __ u __
17. __ e __ a __ a __
18. E __ __ e __
19. __ e __ i
20. __ e __ __ i

Boggler #28

Restoring Consonants, part 2

Restore the correct consonants in the blanks provided and discover a name from the Book of Mormon. *Answers page 81.*

1. __ e __ o __

2. __ __ e __ e __

3. A __ __ i __ i

4. __ a __ o __ i

5. __ e __ u e __

6. __ i __ e o __

7. __ i __ __ i

8. __ i __ __ i

9. __ i __ __ __ u __ e __

10. __ o a __

11. __ o __ e __ __

12. O __ __ e __

13. O __ __ i

14. __ o __ i __ o __

15. __ o __ i a __ __ o __

16. __ o __ __ o __

17. __ u __ e __

18. __ e e __ __ o __

19. __ o __ a __

20. __ a __ i a __

Vowel-less Scripture Mastery

In the following pages you will find a number of Book of Mormon scripture mastery verses that are missing all of their vowels (*a*, *e*, *i*, *o*, *u*, and sometimes *y*). Your challenge is to translate the following bogglers into their scripture mastery scripture by replacing the vowels. The only capitalized letters are those of proper nouns. Letters in bold indicate that there are no missing letters (for example, the word **I** or **a**).

Boggler #29

Vowel-less Scripture Mastery, part 1

Refer to scripture verses listed for answers.

1. (1 Nephi 3:7) I wll g nd d th things whch th Lrd hth cmmndd, fr **I**

knw tht th Lrd gvth n cmmndmnt nt th chldrn f mn, sv h shll prpr **a**

wy fr thm tht thy my ccmplsh th thng whch h cmmndth thm.

2. (1 Nephi 19:23) Fr **I** dd lkn ll scrptrs nt s, tht t mght b fr r

prft nd lrnng.

3. (2 Nephi 2:25) dm fll tht mn mght b; nd mn r, tht thy mght hv jy.

4. (2 Nephi 2:27) Whrfr, mn r fr ccrdng t th flsh; nd ll thngs r gvn thm

whch r xpdnt nt mn. nd thy r fr t chs lbrty nd trnl lf, thrgh th grt

Mdtr f ll mn, r t chs cptvty nd dth, ccrdng t th cptvty nd pwr f th

dvl: fr h skth tht ll mn mght b msrbl lk nt hmslf.

Vowel-less Scripture Mastery, part 2

1. (2 Nephi 9:28–29) O tht cnnng pln f th vl n! O th vnnss,

nd th frlts, nd th flshnss f mn! whn thy r lrnd thy thnk thy r ws,

nd thy hrkn nt nt th cnsl f Gd, fr thy st t sd, sppsng thy knw f

thmslvs, whrfr, thr wsdm s flshnss nd t prftth thm nt. nd thy shll

prsh. bt t b lrnd s gd f thy hrkn nt th cnsls f Gd.

2. (2 Nephi 28:8) Mny whch shll sy; t, drnk, nd b mrry; nvrthlss, fr

G—h wll jstfy n cmmttng a lttl sn; y, l **a** lttl, tk th dvntg f n bcs

f hs wrds, dg **a** pt fr th nghbr; thr s n hrm n ths; nd d ll ths

thngs, fr tmrrw w d; nd f t s b tht w b glty, Gd wll bt s wth **a**

fw strps, nd t lst w shll b svd n th kngdm f Gd.

3. (2 Nephi 32:8–9) Fr f y wld hkn nt th Sprt whch tchth **a** mn t

pry y wld knw tht y mst pry; fr th vl sprt tchth nt **a** mn t pry,

bt tchth hm tht h mst nt pry. ... y mst pry lwys, nd nt fnt; tht y

mst nt prfrm ny thng nt th Lrd sv n th frst plc y shll pry nt th

Fthr n th nm f Chrst, tht h wll cnscrt th prfrmnc nt th, tht th

prfrmnc my b fr th wlfr f th sl.

(Continued on next page)

4. (2 Nephi 32:3) ngls spk b th pwr f th Hly Ghst; whrfr, thy spk th

wrds f Chrst. Whrfr, I sd nt y, fst pn th wrds f Chrst; fr bhld, th

wrds f Chrst wll tll y ll things wht y shld d.

_____

5. (Jacob 2:18) Bt bfr y sk fr rchs, sk y fr th kngdm f Gd.

_____

6. (Mosiah 2:17) Whn y r n th srvc f yr fllw bngs y r nly n th

srvc f yr Gd.

_____

7. (Mosiah 2:17) nd bhld, I tll y ths thngs tht y my lrn wsdm; tht y my

lrn tht whn y r n th srvc of yr fllw bngs y r nly n th srvc f yr Gd.

_____

8. (Mosiah 3:19) Fr th ntrl mn s n nmy t Gd, nd hs bn frm th fll f

dm, nd wll b, frvr nd vr, nlss h ylds t th ntcngs f th Hly Sprt, nd

pttth ff th ntrl mn nd bcmth **a** snt thrgh th tnmnt f Chrst th Lrd,

nd bcmth s **a** chld, sbmssv, mk, hmbl, ptnt, fll f lv, wllng t sbmt t

ll thngs whch th Lrd sth ft t nflct pn hm, vn s **a** chld dth sbmt t

hs fthr.

_____

Vowel-less Scripture Mastery, part 3

1. (Mosiah 4:30) Bt ths mch **I** cn tll y, tht f y d nt wtch yrslvs, nd

_____

yr thghts, nd yr wrds, nd yr dds, nd bsrv th cmmndmnts f Gd,

_____

nd cntn n th fth f wht y hv hrd, cncnng th cmng f r Lrd, vn nt

_____

th nd f yr lvs, y mst prsh. nd nw, **O** mn, rmmber, nd prsh n

_____

2. (Alma 32:21) Fth s nt t hv **a** prfct knwldg f thngs; thrfr f y hv

_____

fth y hp fr thngs whch r nt sn, whch r tr.

_____

3. (Alma 34:33) **I** bsch f y tht y d nt prcrstnt th dy f yr rpntnc ntl

_____

th nd; fr ftr ths dy f lf, whch s gvn u t prpr fr trnty, bhld, f w

_____

d nt mprv r tm whl n ths lf, thn cmth th nght f drknss whrn thr

_____

cn b n lbr prfrmd.

_____

4. (Alma 37:6) B smll nd smpl thngs r grt thngs brght t pss; nd

_____

smll mns n mny nstncs dth cnfnd th ws.

_____

Vowel-less Scripture Mastery, part 4

1. (Alma 37:35) O, rmmbr, m sn, nd lrn wsdm n th yth; y, lrn n th

yth t kp th cmmndmnts f Gd.

2. (Alma 41:10) D nt spps, bcs t hs bn spkn cncrnng rstrtn, tht y shll b

rstrd frm sn t hppnss. Bhld, **I** sy nt y, wckdnss nvr ws hppnss.

3. (Helaman 5:12) nd nw, m sn, rmmber, rmmber, tht t s pn th rck f

r Rdms, wh s Chrst, th Sn f Gd, that y mst bld yr fndtn; tht

whn th dvl shll snd frth hs mghty wnds, y, hs shfts n th whrlwnd,

y, whn ll hs hl nd hs mghty strm shll bt pn y, t shll hv n pwr vr

y t drg y dwn t th glf f msry nd ndllss w, bcs f th rck pn whch

y r blt, whch s **a** sr fndtn, **a** fndtn whrn f mn bld thy cnnt fll.

4. (3 Nephi 11:29) Fr vrly, vrly **I** sy nt y, h tht hth th sprt f cntntn s nt f

m, bt s f th dvl, wh s th fthr f cntntn, nd h strrth p th hrts f mn t cntnd

wth ngr, n wth nthr.

(Continued on next page)

5. (3 Nephi 27:27) nd knw y tht y shll b jdgs f ths ppl, ccrdng t th

jdgmnt whch **I** shll gv nt y, whch shll b jst. Thrfr, wht mnnr f mn

ght y t b? vrly **I** sy nt y, vn s **I** m.

_____

6. (Ether 12:6) **I** wld shw nt th wrld tht fth s thngs whch r hpd fr

nd nt sn; whrfr, dspt nt bcs y s nt, fr y rcv n wtnss ntl ftr th trl f

yr fth.

_____

7. (Ether 12:27) nd f mn cm nt m **I** wll shw nt thm thr wknss. **I** gv

nt mn wknss tht thy my b hmbl; nd m grc s sffcnt fr ll mn tht

hmbl thmslvs bfr m; fr f thy hmbl thmsvls brf m nd hv fth n m,

thn wll **I** mk wk thngs bcm strng nt thm.

_____

Vowel-less Scripture Mastery, part 5

1. (Moroni 7:16–17) Fr bhld, th Sprt f Chrst s gvn t vry mn, tht h my

knw gd frm vl; whrfr, **I** shw nt y th wy t jdg; fr rvy thng whch

nvtth t d gd, nd t prsd t blv n Chrst, s snt frth b th pwr nd gft f

Chrst; whrfr y my knw wth a prfct knwldg t s f Gd. Bt whtsvr

thng prsdth mn t d vl nd blv nt n Chrst, nd dny hm, nd srv nt

Gd, thn y my knw wth **a** prfct knwldg t s f th dvl; fr ftr ths

mnnr dth th dvl wrk, fr h prsdth n mn t d gd, n, nt n; nthr d hs

ngls, nthr d thy wh sbjct thmslvs nt hm.

2. (Moroni 7:45) nd chrty sffrth lng, nd s knd, nd nvth nt, nd s nt

pffd p, skth nt hr wn, s nt sly prvkd, thnkth n vl, nd rjcth nt n

nqty bt rjcth n th trth, brth ll thngs, blvth ll thngs, hpth ll thngs,

ndrth ll things.

(Continued on next page)

3. (Moroni 10:4–5) nd whn y shll rcv ths thngs, **I** wld xhrt y tht y

_____

wld sk Gd, th trnl Fthr, n th nm f Chrst, f ths thngs r nt tr; nd f

_____

y shll sk wth **a** sncr hrt, nd wth rl ntnt, hvng fth n Chrst, h wl

_____

mnfst th trth f t nt y, b th pwr f th Hly Ghst. nd b th pwr f th

_____

Hly Ghst y my knw th trth f ll thngs.

_____

Word Search Bogglers

A ll of the words in these next bogglers have been taken from the scriptures and hidden in word searches. How fast can you find them all?

Boggler #30

Word Search #1

All of the words found in this word search were taken from 2 Nephi 28. Can you find the following words? *Answers page 82.*

remnant, house, church, contend, learning, precepts, miracle, eat, drink, merry, die, fear, justify, committing, sins, dig, pit, guilty, foolish, doctrine, hide, counsels, works, dark, rob, poor, persecute, meek, thrust, down

R	P	D	K	O	B	G	D	M	L	M	C	S	P	Z	D	M	N	R	H
N	E	V	H	G	Q	A	W	H	E	S	T	M	O	B	V	P	O	O	R
J	R	M	E	E	K	A	A	D	A	R	K	Z	X	C	O	J	U	B	B
B	S	N	N	V	B	N	J	E	R	W	O	R	J	H	F	S	H	M	T
K	E	K	B	A	L	H	G	F	N	D	B	M	O	M	E	D	M	B	A
L	C	O	K	I	N	O	L	D	I	E	M	B	I	W	V	N	H	Y	I
M	U	P	L	L	K	T	V	Z	N	X	H	T	E	W	A	I	C	T	F
F	T	T	P	Y	G	Y	M	N	G	U	I	L	T	Y	L	F	V	I	M
K	E	S	I	T	O	C	N	P	P	Z	D	X	N	B	R	W	Z	L	M
C	B	Z	E	R	I	C	O	U	N	S	E	L	S	V	C	V	Q	R	I
H	J	B	R	C	O	M	M	I	T	T	I	N	G	K	N	F	E	A	R
U	F	Q	B	V	Y	R	T	H	R	U	S	T	E	D	T	L	H	F	A
R	W	P	S	C	T	I	V	W	A	S	U	B	K	V	O	V	I	M	C
C	X	O	I	B	P	N	I	U	B	N	V	E	L	K	O	W	Q	A	L
H	I	T	K	C	V	G	W	M	E	R	R	Y	B	V	U	K	N	M	E
C	B	G	D	R	I	N	K	U	N	R	F	X	K	E	L	S	I	N	S
E	A	T	B	D	Q	V	S	M	C	N	U	F	N	M	H	M	B	I	V
C	X	R	T	B	N	T	B	H	G	C	U	I	D	B	R	E	Y	Q	Y
X	G	O	V	U	P	K	H	S	L	B	R	E	C	N	W	I	V	R	O
B	Y	J	L	E	D	B	D	I	I	T	T	H	N	J	E	N	S	E	Z
D	V	H	C	X	K	M	U	L	C	F	N	K	J	U	S	T	I	F	Y
C	W	E	B	J	B	E	N	O	V	J	T	E	G	F	X	R	N	P	Y
R	R	O	N	O	P	X	D	O	Q	R	N	L	V	D	H	X	R	O	T
P	O	K	L	M	L	P	R	F	O	H	G	R	D	C	W	M	W	L	C

Boggler #31

Word Search #2

All of the words found in this word search are taken from Mosiah 2 and 3. Can you find the following words? *Answers page 83.*

natural, enemy, yields, enticings, meek, love, submit, pain,
fire, anguish, indebted, peace, requires, commandments,
tower, service, lending, serve, indebted, immortal, guilt,
mercy, saint, inflict, profitable

```
A  D  C  J  U  G  P  M  G  Y  G  M  C  E  Z  B  O  C  Q  K
B  E  I  I  A  K  O  N  B  M  N  V  M  N  H  K  L  O  V  E
E  P  A  I  N  D  I  N  A  T  U  R  A  L  S  V  C  M  X  M
N  Y  V  L  K  D  J  E  N  E  B  T  L  I  K  G  N  M  O  V
T  E  A  D  N  J  G  Y  V  P  E  M  O  Q  W  Y  C  A  O  P
I  F  F  E  D  I  N  D  E  B  T  E  D  W  O  V  N  N  L  K
C  W  L  K  A  T  I  L  U  X  L  W  E  B  E  M  J  D  Q  O
I  S  D  B  I  N  A  L  N  Z  E  X  M  Y  D  R  T  M  H  H
N  V  N  I  P  T  G  G  W  C  E  Z  T  K  N  B  M  E  E  K
G  B  C  H  R  M  V  U  H  R  W  A  L  N  A  C  L  N  K  G
S  B  V  O  E  M  D  S  I  V  M  T  I  U  P  K  T  T  R  E
A  Y  M  R  N  N  Y  F  C  S  C  L  U  J  V  T  B  S  B  N
D  M  C  Z  E  E  U  M  O  N  H  R  G  R  W  S  N  F  T  Y
I  U  M  D  M  E  P  R  O  F  I  T  A  B  L  E  T  I  B  B
U  Y  R  A  Y  W  I  J  P  S  V  U  F  D  I  L  X  U  A  N
A  Z  G  K  E  Y  O  P  Y  I  E  L  D  S  A  D  G  E  M  S
T  E  Q  A  Z  C  T  V  M  L  J  R  G  F  S  Z  C  C  E  B
U  O  P  Z  V  C  N  T  U  O  P  R  V  B  V  A  T  R  G  J
R  E  Q  U  I  R  E  S  D  W  S  W  U  I  E  U  I  O  L  Q
E  R  T  L  H  J  K  U  L  M  Z  X  C  P  C  U  B  Y  U  G
A  S  F  F  T  D  B  B  Y  U  K  R  N  W  Q  E  Z  V  N  O
C  N  B  M  G  T  Y  M  I  D  V  W  G  E  G  S  E  R  V  E
I  F  D  F  J  N  G  I  D  A  Q  I  R  M  N  G  M  Y  O  K
K  Y  I  N  D  E  B  T  E  D  A  U  G  N  K  M  E  R  C  Y
```

Boggler #32

Word Search #3

All of the words found in this word search were taken from 2 Nephi 2. Can you find the following words? *Answers page 84.*

redeemed, righteousness, fullness, fall, temporal, spiritual, forever, miserable, flesh, resurrection, dead, first, rise, punishment, opposition, happiness, wickedness, holiness, grace, misery, good, bad, choose, free, liberty, life, innocence

```
S  F  H  K  G  Y  B  F  B  M  L  S  G  R  A  C  E  Z  V  G
F  R  S  A  O  P  R  T  R  E  C  O  A  F  J  R  G  T  S  D
G  E  V  B  O  F  V  B  Q  P  P  H  O  R  A  S  L  G  J  G
F  D  E  A  D  L  K  H  A  P  P  I  N  E  S  S  D  F  K  T
F  E  Y  D  S  F  J  T  O  F  X  L  K  E  G  U  M  N  S  B
G  E  J  V  L  D  S  S  F  B  V  C  B  N  Z  Q  D  R  Q  W
D  M  F  G  D  L  I  B  E  R  T  Y  P  O  I  Y  I  T  R  E
C  E  X  C  F  T  D  M  N  V  L  K  J  S  H  F  G  H  R  P
R  D  T  U  I  Q  F  U  L  L  N  E  S  S  E  R  T  Y  I  U
S  R  E  O  D  S  A  E  G  T  T  E  N  P  F  S  J  K  O  N
H  C  N  X  R  U  L  F  G  W  N  B  M  I  H  M  I  G  L  I
O  D  W  U  Y  E  L  H  D  S  M  F  O  R  E  V  E  R  F  S
L  I  F  E  C  W  B  H  U  Q  I  K  H  I  G  H  I  J  M  H
I  K  Z  O  V  B  M  O  S  A  S  O  S  T  D  F  C  N  B  M
N  J  X  M  I  S  E  R  Y  U  E  J  E  U  S  G  H  R  I  E
E  H  S  D  F  T  E  M  P  O  R  A  L  A  A  F  O  J  N  N
S  L  D  F  H  J  K  Q  L  Q  A  W  F  L  E  R  O  T  N  T
S  D  A  G  S  D  F  H  G  K  B  J  L  N  V  C  S  B  O  N
Q  N  I  L  P  O  I  U  T  E  L  Q  A  S  S  F  E  G  C  H
A  R  W  X  V  C  W  I  C  K  E  D  N  E  S  S  X  C  E  V
Z  V  M  H  F  A  Q  E  T  U  M  V  B  M  I  Q  F  H  N  B
X  B  R  E  S  U  R  R  E  C  T  I  O  N  T  A  J  F  C  N
C  N  J  G  D  S  W  R  Y  I  O  D  H  P  F  D  K  T  E  F
```

51

Boggler #33

Word Search #4

All of the names in the puzzle below are found in the Book of Mormon. Can you find the names listed below? *Answers page 85.*

Jacob, Amos, Nephihah, Samuel, Jarom, Amulon, Ammoron, Akish, Amalickiah, Aaron, Abish, Isaiah, Kishkumen, Enos, Gadianton, Omni, Hagoth, Laban, Shiz, Abinadi, Alma, Ammon, Ishmael, Jared, Ether, Giddonah, Gideon, Helam, Helaman, Shiblon, Teancum

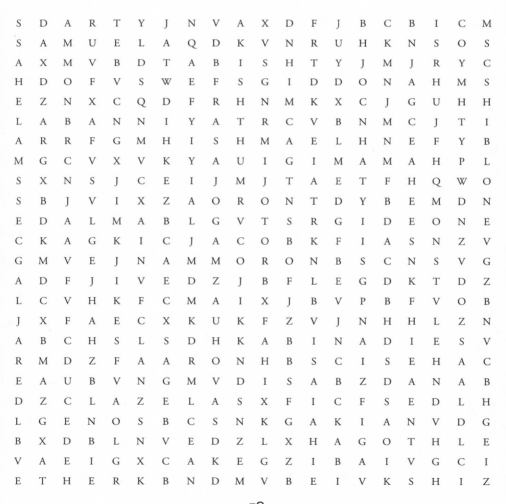

```
S  D  A  R  T  Y  J  N  V  A  X  D  F  J  B  C  B  I  C  M
S  A  M  U  E  L  A  Q  D  K  V  N  R  U  H  K  N  S  O  S
A  X  M  V  B  D  T  A  B  I  S  H  T  Y  J  M  J  R  Y  C
H  D  O  F  V  S  W  E  F  S  G  I  D  D  O  N  A  H  M  S
E  Z  N  X  C  Q  D  F  R  H  N  M  K  X  C  J  G  U  H  H
L  A  B  A  N  N  I  Y  A  T  R  C  V  B  N  M  C  J  T  I
A  R  R  F  G  M  H  I  S  H  M  A  E  L  H  N  E  F  Y  B
M  G  C  V  X  V  K  Y  A  U  I  G  I  M  A  M  A  H  P  L
S  X  N  S  J  C  E  I  J  M  J  T  A  E  T  F  H  Q  W  O
S  B  J  V  I  X  Z  A  O  R  O  N  T  D  Y  B  E  M  D  N
E  D  A  L  M  A  B  L  G  V  T  S  R  G  I  D  E  O  N  E
C  K  A  G  K  I  C  J  A  C  O  B  K  F  I  A  S  N  Z  V
G  M  V  E  J  N  A  M  M  O  R  O  N  B  S  C  N  S  V  G
A  D  F  J  I  V  E  D  Z  J  B  F  L  E  G  D  K  T  D  Z
L  C  V  H  K  F  C  M  A  I  X  J  B  V  P  B  F  V  O  B
J  X  F  A  E  C  X  K  U  K  F  Z  V  J  N  H  H  L  Z  N
A  B  C  H  S  L  S  D  H  K  A  B  I  N  A  D  I  E  S  V
R  M  D  Z  F  A  A  R  O  N  H  B  S  C  I  S  E  H  A  C
E  A  U  B  V  N  G  M  V  D  I  S  A  B  Z  D  A  N  A  B
D  Z  C  L  A  Z  E  L  A  S  X  F  I  C  F  S  E  D  L  H
L  G  E  N  O  S  B  C  S  N  K  G  A  K  I  A  N  V  D  G
B  X  D  B  L  N  V  E  D  Z  L  X  H  A  G  O  T  H  L  E
V  A  E  I  G  X  C  A  K  E  G  Z  I  B  A  I  V  G  C  I
E  T  H  E  R  K  B  N  D  M  V  B  E  I  V  K  S  H  I  Z
```

Boggler #34

Word Search #5

In the Book of Mormon, there are over forty different names that refer to Jesus Christ. Can you find those different names listed below in this puzzle? *Answers page 86.*

Son of God, Beloved Son, Holy Child, Shepherd, Savior,
Maker, Messiah, Lamb, Holy One of Jacob, Only Begotten Son,
The Very Christ, Jehovah, Lord, Jesus Christ, Heavenly King,
Eternal God, Holy One, Lamb of God, Father, Holy One of Israel,
Lord Omnipotent, Redeemer

H	M	H	E	A	X	J	E	H	O	V	A	H	K	U	F	B	C	P	L
M	R	A	C	X	H	C	P	M	Y	B	G	V	C	F	C	Q	W	O	O
G	N	I	K	Y	L	N	E	V	A	E	H	V	X	A	H	B	R	V	N
G	I	P	L	E	B	N	T	D	C	N	K	J	H	T	D	D	T	Y	L
K	L	P	O	A	R	C	L	Z	X	T	E	W	A	H	J	G	U	I	Y
L	K	H	F	O	A	I	J	H	G	D	S	T	Y	E	I	P	L	J	B
N	B	Y	I	V	H	C	X	D	N	Y	G	H	S	R	F	D	E	Y	E
L	P	V	O	C	K	J	H	O	G	F	D	U	A	S	E	R	W	E	G
T	A	H	Y	H	T	Y	S	V	G	S	S	M	L	O	P	A	S	D	O
S	V	L	X	M	F	D	T	H	E	V	E	R	Y	C	H	R	I	S	T
C	O	M	O	R	E	D	E	E	M	E	R	X	Y	I	L	P	F	Y	T
H	S	N	S	V	J	U	Y	R	E	D	O	G	L	A	N	R	E	T	E
P	O	L	O	R	D	O	M	N	I	P	O	T	E	N	T	N	H	V	N
A	E	L	B	F	C	G	F	U	L	O	P	L	H	U	E	T	D	G	S
N	E	V	B	Y	G	C	X	R	E	A	B	H	A	X	Y	T	R	E	O
B	N	M	C	G	T	O	C	V	X	R	M	L	K	I	O	U	Y	E	N
S	H	E	P	H	E	R	D	J	I	K	E	B	Q	T	H	U	I	T	Y
C	W	S	N	U	G	Y	T	N	T	N	M	O	O	V	S	Z	E	D	F
M	O	S	B	T	G	D	E	R	O	N	B	U	H	F	V	I	X	Z	D
B	U	I	N	I	K	L	O	Y	P	O	I	B	Z	D	G	V	R	X	C
V	G	A	T	F	R	E	L	B	H	J	J	M	N	B	J	O	M	H	V
V	Y	H	O	L	Y	O	N	E	O	F	J	A	C	O	B	N	D	O	C
B	H	U	T	O	H	Z	K	J	H	J	I	L	J	N	N	G	X	F	O
A	M	H	O	L	Y	O	N	E	O	F	I	S	R	A	E	L	C	F	U

Groupie Bogglers

In the Book of Mormon, there are many groups of important people and things. The following bogglers will challenge you to separate lists of people and items into categories. Use the scriptures to help you identify which items belong in each group.

Boggler #35

Groupie #1: "Metal Works"

The following words can be gathered into four unique groups, listed below. Can you identify the groups and then place the words into the proper group? *Answers page 87.*

buckler, dagger, breastplates, onti, copper,
seon, bow, shield, limnah, ziff, cimeters, iron

Groups: armor, money, metals, weapons

Group #1: _____

1. _____

2. _____

3. _____

Group #2: _____

1. _____

2. _____

3. _____

Group #3: _____

1. _____

2. _____

3. _____

Group #4: _____

1. _____

2. _____

3. _____

Boggler #36

Groupie #2: "Name those Plates"

The following names can be categorized into unique groups, listed below. Can you place the names into their proper groups? *Answers page 87.*

Mosiah, Enos, Mormon, Jarom, Moroni, Jacob,
Alma, Lehi, Jeremiah, Ether, Isaiah, Exodus

Groups: large plates, small plates, brass plates, plates of Mormon

Group #1: _____
1. _____
2. _____
3. _____

Group #2: _____
1. _____
2. _____
3. _____

Group #3: _____
1. _____
2. _____
3. _____

Group #4: _____
1. _____
2. _____
3. _____

Boggler #37

Groupie #3: "Brother, Where Art Thou?"

The following names are sons of Book of Mormon characters. Can you identify their groups (listed below) and place the names into their proper categories? *Answers page 87.*

Sam, Helorum, Helaman, Omner, Aaron, Shiblon,
Laman, Corianton, Jacob, Mosiah, Helaman, Himni

Groups: sons of Lehi, sons of Mosiah,
sons of Alma the Younger, sons of Benjamin

Group #1: _____
1. _____
2. _____
3. _____

Group #2: _____
1. _____
2. _____
3. _____

Group #3: _____
1. _____
2. _____
3. _____

Group #4: _____
1. _____
2. _____
3. _____

Boggler #38

Groupie #4: "Family Ties—Father and Son"

The following names can be grouped into families. Can you identify their lineage and place the names into their proper groups? *Answers page 87.*

Alma, Mosiah, Omner, Shiblon, Corianton, Ammon,
Pahoran, Joseph, Lehi, Pacumeni, Jacob, Paanchi

Groups: Alma and sons, Mosiah and sons,
Pahoran and sons, Lehi and sons

Group #1: _____
1. _____
2. _____
3. _____

Group #2: _____
1. _____
2. _____
3. _____

Group #3: _____
1. _____
2. _____
3. _____

Group #4: _____
1. _____
2. _____
3. _____

Boggler #39

Groupie #5: "Kings and Chief Judges"

The names below are Book of Mormon leaders. Can you place the names into their proper groups? *Answers page 87.*

Mosiah, Laman, Nephi, Kib, Alma, Helaman, Amalickiah, Benjamin, Coriantumr, Lachoneus, Lamoni, Orihah

Groups: Jaredite kings, Nephite kings, chief judges, Lamanite kings

Group #1: _____

1. _____
2. _____
3. _____

Group #2: _____

1. _____
2. _____
3. _____

Group #3: _____

1. _____
2. _____
3. _____

Group #4: _____

1. _____
2. _____
3. _____

Scrambler Bogglers

The next pages are full of words from specific chapters in the Book of Mormon, but the letters are all mixed up! Reorganize the letters to figure out what the original scripture word is.

Boggler #40

Scrambler #1

Can you unscramble the words listed below? They can all be found in Moroni 6 and 7. *Answers page 88.*

tpaziebd   _____

okrenb   _____

notctrei   _____

setwidens   _____

rvees   _____

nlcseeda   _____

rcchuh   _____

sfta   _____

hracyti   _____

cpabeleae   _____

fitg   _____

gudje   _____

eadsreup   _____

evlbeie   _____

krwo   _____

githl   _____

leiv   _____

arsilmce   _____

phoe   _____

ekem   _____

Boggler #41

Scrambler #2

Can you unscramble the words listed below? All of the scramblers here are found in Alma 34. *Answers page 88.*

etnoa _____

rspihe _____

stol _____

ifsaricec _____

tniiifne _____

tmaoteenn _____

ntelare _____

remyc _____

itsfasy _____

mdneasd _____

stjciue _____

scxireee _____

ssni _____

npeneteacr _____

esav _____

yrpear _____

pmirta _____

awl _____

csaportrnitea _____

eparrep _____

Boggler #42

Scrambler #3

Can you unscramble the words listed below? All of the scramblers here are found in Alma 32. *Answers page 88.*

rwhopsi _____

eldhbum _____

ynaggsoeus _____

lopcmdlee _____

hudnetre _____

ahitf _____

umcfeilr _____

metnxepire _____

rsidee _____

dntapel _____

orwg _____

esde _____

rateh _____

lwsel _____

lengtihne _____

gnearle _____

rsohuin _____

ufitr _____

gnleetc _____

drwo _____

Boggler #43

Scrambler #4

Can you unscramble the words listed below? All of the scramblers listed below are names of characters found in the Book of Mormon. *Answers page 88.*

raona   _____

ibdaina   _____

baihs   _____

mlaa   _____

peshoj   _____

ojnsa   _____

emorn   _____

iohkror   _____

uencmta   _____

milcai   _____

banal   _____

mukne   _____

hhhaipen   _____

shmnkeiku   _____

roinmo   _____

ajmbnein   _____

mlaan   _____

anho   _____

cjabo   _____

mmroon   _____

Boggler #44

Scrambler #5

C an you unscramble the words listed below? All of the scramblers listed below are names of characters found in the Book of Mormon. *Answers page 88–89.*

nmamora   _____

zhis   _____

mnmao   _____

heil   _____

redja   _____

nblsiho   _____

ionm   _____

aaahiiclkm   _____

nolmai   _____

mjrao   _____

mlaeika   _____

uelmle   _____

ocatnnoir   _____

rnoahap   _____

osne   _____

bli   _____

hgtoah   _____

ilaimc   _____

rsaiha   _____

ogeidn   _____

Boggler #45

Scrambler #6

Can you unscramble the words listed below? All of the scramblers listed below are names of characters found in the Book of Mormon. *Answers page 89.*

smoa   _____

msa   _____

slhieam   _____

ehsrem   _____

hetre   _____

ulakem   _____

lumke   _____

nmraao   _____

bki   _____

shichme   _____

pineh   _____

idgatnona   _____

ohna   _____

moamnor   _____

tohmnia   _____

imhli   _____

enorh   _____

lsmaeu   _____

shoiam   _____

Picture Script Bogglers

On the following pages you will find images that convey the messages of certain scriptural phrases. Your challenge is to determine the scriptural phrase by studying the images. No answer key is provided, but you can find the answer by reading the scriptural reference listed below the images.

favored

of

the Lord

1 Nephi 1:1

1 Nephi 1:13

DESIRES
2 no
mist
of God

1 Nephi 2:16

1st land
land
land
land

1 Nephi 2:20

STATURE

1 Nephi 2:16

Ruler **&** *Teacher*

---

brothers

1 Nephi 2:22

1 Nephi 2:16

1 Nephi 3:11

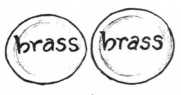

1 Nephi 3:3

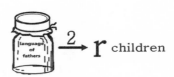

1 Nephi 3:19

1 Nephi 4:6

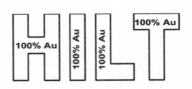

1 Nephi 4:9

1 Nephi 8:24

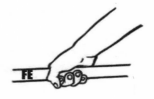

1 Nephi 8:30

1 Nephi 13:33

1 Nephi 13:37

1 Nephi 16:29

1 Nephi 17:2

1 Nephi 17:42

1 Nephi 22:25

unbelief

2 Nephi 1:10

2 Nephi 1:17

2 Nephi 2:7

born (born)

2 Nephi 3:1

speamightyking

2 Nephi 3:17

2 Nephi 4:15

2 Nephi 4:35

2 Nephi 4:3

2 Nephi 28:3

2 Nephi 9:15

2 Nephi 9:30

2 Nephi 9:34

2 Nephi 28:32

2 Nephi 31:20

2 Nephi 33:11

2 Nephi 30:13

2 Nephi 32:1

Enos 1:3

slaborin

Jacob 2:5

Enos 1:11

Words of Mormon 1:17

Mosiah 11:2

Jarom 1:12

Mosiah 2:41

Mosiah 3:3

Mosiah 21:13

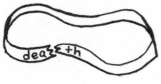

Mosiah 15:9

Mosiah 16:7

Mosiah 23:13

Alma 5:52

Alma 1:6

Alma 5:15

Alma 5:44

Alma 5:45

Alma 6:1

Alma 8:14

Alma 17:29

Alma 34:38

Answer Key

Boggler #1—Numbers, part 1

1. 600
2. 3
3. 50
4. 50, 10's, 1000's
5. 5
6. 5
7. 600
8. 2
9. 2
10. 2
11. 4
12. 1
13. 8
14. 2
15. 2
16. 4
17. 1, 1
18. 4
19. 30

Boggler #1—Number, part 2

20. 3
21. 600
22. 3
23. 2
24. 1
25. 9
26. 30
27. 16
28. 40
29. 2
30. ½
31. 43
32. 24
33. 2
34. 204
35. 1, 50
36. 450
37. 24
38. 2
39. 8
40. 12

Boggler #1—Number, part 3

41. 7
42. 2
43. 4
44. 82
45. 63
46. 3500
47. 91
48. 9
49. 6
50. 1
51. 14
52. 3
53. 6
54. 1
55. 1
56. 2, 2
57. 1
58. 1
59. 1½
60. 1, 0

Boggler #2—Book of Mormon comes forth

1. AD 421
2. Sept. 1823
3. Sept. 1827
4. July 1828
5. April 1829
6. Nov. 1829
7. Aug. 1829
8. June 1829
9. Feb. 1828
10. June 1828
11. Aug. 1829

Boggler #3—Book of Mormon Birthdays

1.	G	5.	A	9.	E
2.	I	6.	C	10.	L
3.	K	7.	D	11.	B
4.	H	8.	F	12.	J

Boggler #4—Pages, Pages

1.	E	6.	M	11.	H
2.	I	7.	K	12.	A
3.	A	8.	D	13.	C
4.	L	9.	B	14.	J
5.	G	10.	F		

Boggler #5—Time in a Book

1.	H	6.	M	11.	C
2.	K	7.	B	12.	I
3.	A	8.	D	13.	F
4.	E	9.	L		
5.	J	10.	G		

Boggler #6—Alma Who?

1.	B	5.	A	9.	A
2.	A	6.	B	10.	A
3.	B	7.	B	11.	A
4.	B	8.	A	12.	B

Boggler #7—Scripture Plates

1.	B	5.	A	9.	C
2.	A	6.	E	10.	A
3.	C	7.	B	11.	B
4.	D	8.	E		

Boggler #8—Keeper of the Record

1.	Lehi	6.	Omni	11.	Benjamin
2.	Nephi	7.	Amaron	12.	Mosiah (2)
3.	Jacob	8.	Chemish	13.	Alma (2)
4.	Enos	9.	Abinadom	14.	Helaman (2)
5.	Jarom	10.	Amaleki	15.	Shiblon

Boggler #9—Family Business

1. C	5. C	9. A
2. B	6. A	10. C
3. D	7. A	11. A
4. C	8. B	

Boggler #10—Kings in the Book of Mormon

1. F	6. D	11. B
2. D	7. C	12. A
3. A	8. B	13. E
4. E	9. F	14. C
5. G	10. G	

Boggler #11—Roaming in the Wilderness

1. E	5. K	9. L
2. B	6. A	10. H
3. I	7. J	11. D
4. G	8. C	12. F

Boggler #12—Doctrinal Message Search

1. E	6. L	11. A
2. N	7. H	12. I
3. G	8. C	13. F
4. B	9. K	14. O
5. J	10. M	15. D

Boggler #13—Doctrinal Message Search, part 2

1. D	6. A	11. G
2. H	7. N	12. C
3. E	8. M	13. O
4. J	9. B	14. I
5. K	10. L	15. F

Boggler #14—Doctrinal Message Search, part 3

1. L	7. E	13. C
2. G	8. J	14. K
3. O	9. D	15. I
4. A	10. N	
5. M	11. H	
6. B	12. F	

Boggler # 15—Disbelievers

1. B	7. B	13. C
2. D	8. A	14. C
3. B	9. D	15. D
4. A	10. A	16. C
5. C	11. B	
6. D	12. A	

Boggler # 16—Disbelivers: Who said That

1. A	4. C	7. D
2. D	5. C	8. A
3. B	6. B	

Boggler #17—The Devil Made Me Do It

1. merry, die	5. no	9. rob
2. little, advantage	6. power	10. stiff, high
3. pit	7. learning, deny	
4. miracles, work	8. puffed, hid	

Boggler #18—The Faith Experiment

1. cause, knoweth	6. arouse, experiment,	10. nourishment, root
2. perfect	particle	11. faith, forward, ,root,
3. hope, not	7. seed	everlasting
4. cursed	8. heart, true, cast, swell	
5. compelled	9. likeness	

Boggler #19—Procrastinate?

1. mankind, perish	6. sacrifice, mercy, overpowereth,
2. last, man, fowl, human, infinite, eternal	repentance
3. sacrifice, atone	7. mercy, justice
4. short, suffice, world	8. faith, exposed
5. pointing, Son, God	9. life, prepare, meet
	10. procrastinate, death

Boggler #20—Opposition Needed?

1. must	sin
2. forbidden, tree, bitter	8. free
3. act	9. choose
4. die, knowing , evil	10. miserable
5. partaken, driven	
6. remained, created, same, forever	
7. children, innocence, joy, good,	

Boggler #21—Tell Me What Will Happen

1. all, forth
2. time
3. righteous, happiness, paradise, rest, troubles
4. part, chose, good
5. darkness, fiery, remain, time
6. reuniting
7. body, soul, joint, restored, hair, lost

Boggler #22—Mercy, Mercy

1. temporally, spiritually, will
2. reclaimed, spiritual
3. means, disobedience
4. redemption, repentance
5. destroy, destroyed, cease
6. mankind, grasp
7. mercy, atonement, atoneth, appease, just, merciful
8. penitent
9. resurrection
10. demands, her, none, saved

Boggler #23—Restoring Vowels

1. Moses
2. Lachoneus
3. Nephihah
4. Nehor
5. Moroni
6. Helorum
7. Jarom
8. Lehi
9. Giddonah
10. Abinadi
11. Amilici
12. Gadianton
13. Aaron
14. Kumen
15. Ammon
16. Mormon
17. Neum
18. Mosiah
19. Jonas

Boggler # 24—Restoring Vowels

1. Helaman
2. Amos
3. Lamoni
4. Ceezoram
5. Gidgiddoni
6. Joseph
7. Amulon
8. Hagoth
9. Kishkumen
10. Antipus
11. Com
12. Adam
13. Benjamin
14. Hlam
15. Laman
16. Abish
17. Gideon
18. Kish
19. Amulek
20. Chemish

Boggler # 25—Restoring Vowels

1. Coriantumr
2. Hem
3. Jacob
4. Alma
5. Mulek
6. Ether
7. Morianton
8. Amaron
9. Lemuel
10. Himni
11. Laan
12. Eve
13. Limhi
14. Helam
15. Amalickiah
16. Enos
17. Ishmael
18. Jared
19. Korihor
20. Coriantum

Boggler # **26**—Restoring Vowels

1. Omner
2. Pacumeni
3. Shweem
4. Pahpran
5. Sarah
6. Zeniff
7. Seezoram
8. Pachus
9. Shiblom
10. Samuel
11. Shemnon
12. Zeezrom
13. Paanchi
14. Seth
15. Sam
16. Nimrod
17. Zedekiah
18. Sariah
19. Noah
20. Pagag

Boggler # **27**—Restoring Consonants

1. Sam
2. Aaron
3. Amaron
4. Amaleki
5. Jared
6. Abish
7. Abinadi
8. Gadianton
9. Ammon
10. Amos
11. Hagoth
12. Amulek
13. Amulon
14. Sammel
15. Helam
16. Teancum
17. Healman
18. Ether
19. Lehi
20. Nephi

Boggler # **28**—Restoring Consonants

1. Nehor
2. Sherem
3. Amlici
4. Lamoni
5. Lemuel
6. Gideon
7. Limhi
8. Himni
9. Kishkumen
10. Noah
11. Joseph
12. Omner
13. Omni
14. Korihor
15. Coriantor
16. Morman
17. Mulek
18. Zeezrom
19. Zoram
20. Sariah

Boggler # **30**—Word Search for the Seekers #**1**

```
R  P                   L                        R  H
   E                   E  S                   P  O  O  R
   R  M  E  E  K        D  A  R  K                U  B
   S     N              R        R           S
   E        A           N              O     E  D
   C           N        D  I  E              W
   U              T     N        H
   T                    G  U  I  L  T  Y
   E                    D                              M
,C                 C  O  U  N  S  E  L  S              I
 H           C  O  M  M  I  T  T  I  N  G     F  E  A  R
 U              T  H  R  U  S  T  E  D              A
 R              I                    O              C
 C           P                          W          L
 H           G     M  E  R  R  Y           N       E
       D  R  I  N  K                 E     S  I  N  S
 E  A  T     D        S                 N
             T     H              I  D
          P        S        R        N
          E        I     T              E
       C           L  C           J  U  S  T  I  F  Y
    E              O                       N
    R              D  O                       O
```

Boggler #31—Word Search #2

```
                        G                           C
                  N                           L   O   V   E
E   P   A   I   N       I   N   A   T   U   R   A   L       M
N               D                       T                   M
T           N                               O               A
I           E       I   N   D   E   B   T   E   D   W       N
C   L       A           L                           E       D
I           N   A                               R           M
N           T   G                   E       T           M   E   E   K
G       R           U       R           L               N
S       O   E               I           I               T
    M   N               F       S           U       T   S
M       E                   H       G           N
I       M       P   R   O   F   I   T   A   B   L   E       I
        Y                   S                               A
                Y   I   E   L   D   S               E       S
            T                   R                   C       E
            C                       V           A   R
R   E   Q   U   I   R   E   S               I   E   I
        L               U               P   C   U
    F               B               Q   E
N               M               E   S   E   R   V   E
I               I           R
    I   N   D   E   B   T   E   D           M   E   R   C   Y
```

83

Boggler #32—Word Search #3

```
            G                       G   R   A   C   E
    R           O               O   A   F
    E       B   O           P   H       R
    D   E   A   D       H   A   P   P   I   N   E   S   S               T
    E       D               O               E                   S
    E                   S                               R
    M           L   I   B   E   R   T   Y                   I
    E           T                       S       F               P
    D       I       F   U   L   L   N   E   S   S   E           U
        O           A   A               E       P       S       N
H       N           L   M           N           I           I   I
O                   L   L       S   M   F   O   R   E   V   E   R   S
L                           U       I       H   I               H
I                           O       S       S   T       C       M
N       M   I   S   E   R   Y       E       E   U       H       I   E
E           T   E   M   P   O   R   A   L   A       O       N   N
S           H                       A       F   L       O       T
S       G                           B               S       O
    I                               L               E       C
    R               W   I   C   K   E   D   N   E   S   S       N
                                                            E
        R   E   S   U   R   R   E   C   T   I   O   N       C
                                                            E
```

84

Boggler # **33**—Word Search #**4**

```
        A                       A                               I       M
S   A   M   U   A   L           K                           N       O
        M                   A   B   I   S   H           M       R
H   O                           S   G   I   D   D   O   N   A   H   M   S
E   N                           H                       J       U           H
L   A   B   A   N               A                           C           I
A                       I   S   H   M   A   E   L           N           B
M                   K       A               G           A               L
                C           M               A   E                       O
            I       A   A   R   O   N   T   D                           N
        A   L   M   A                   S       G   I   D   E   O   N
        A               J   A   C   O   B               A
    M           N   A   M   M   O   R   O   N               N
A                   E                           E           T
            H           M                   P               O
J               E           U                   H               N
A               L       K   A   B   I   N   A   D   I
R   M           A   A   R   O   N   H       S               H
E   U                   M               S   A                   A
D           L               A           I                           H
        E   N   O   S           N           A   K
                N                       H   A   G   O   T   H

E   T   H   E   R                               S   H   I   Z
```

Boggler #34—Word Search #5

```
    M                 J   E   H   O   V   A   H                                 L
      A                                               F                   O
G   N   I   K   Y   L   N   E   V   A   E   H           A               R       N
          E                   D                         T           D           L
            R           L                               H   J                   Y
              O       I                                 E                       B
          I       H               N               S   R                         E
        V       C               O               U                               G
      A       Y             S               S                                   O
S       L           D   T   H   E   V   E   R   Y   C   H   R   I   S           T
  O               R   E   D   E   E   M   E   R                                 T
H     N       V                   D   O   G   L   A   N   R   E   T             E
    L   O   R   D   O   M   N   I   P   O   T   E   N   T                       N
    L       F                   L                                               S
  E               G               A                                             O
B   M                   O               M                                       N
S   H   E   P   H   E   R   D               E   B           T
    S                               N               O       S
    S                           O                   F       I
    I                   Y               B           G   R
    A                 L             M                   O   H
    H   O   L   Y   O   N   E   O   F   J   A   C   O   B       D       C
            H                           L
    H   O   L   Y   O   N   E   O   F   I   S   R   A   E   L
```

Boggler #35—"Metal Works"

Armor
buckler
shield
breast plate
Money
onti

seon
limna
Metals
ziff
iron
copper

Weapons
cimeters
dagger
bow

Boggler #36—"Name those Plates"

Large plates
Mosiah
Lehi
Alma
Small plates
Enos

Jacob
Jarom
Brass plates
Isaiah
Jeremiah
Exodus

Plates of Mormon
Mormon
Moroni
Ether

Boggler #37—"Brother where art Thou?'

Sons of Lehi
Sam
Laman
Jacob
Sons of Mosiah
Himni

Omner
Aaron
Sons of Alma
Helaman
Shiblon
Corianton

Sons of Benjamin
Helorum
Mosiah
Helaman

Boggler #38—"Family Ties" Father/Sons

Alma and Sons
Alma
Shiblon
Corianton
Mosiah and Sons
Mosiah

Ammon
Omner
Pahoran and Sons
Pahoran
Pacumeni
Paanchi

Lehi and Sons
Lehi
Jacob
Joseph

Boggler #39—Kings and Chief Judges

Chief Judges
Alma
Helaman
Lachoneus
Nephite kings
Nephi

Benjamin
Mosiah
Lamanite Kings
Lamoni
Laman
Amalickiah

Jaredite Kings
Orihah
Kib
Coriantumr

87

Boggler #40—Scrambler #1

1. baptized
2. broken
3. contrite
4. witnessed
5. serve
6. cleansed
7. church
8. fast
9. charity
10. peaceable
11. gift
12. judge
13. persuade
14. believe
15. work
16. light
17. evil
18. miracles
19. hope
20. meek

Boggler #41—Scrambler #2

1. atone
2. perish
3. lost
4. sacrifice
5. infinite
6. atonement
7. eternal
8. mercy
9. satisfy
10. demands
11. justice
12. exercised
13. sins
14. repentance
15. save
16. prayer
17. impart
18. law
19. procrastinate
20. prepare

Boggler #42—Scrambler #3

1. worship
2. humbled
3. synagogues
4. compelled
5. endureth
6. faith
7. merciful
8. experiment
9. desire
10. planted
11. grow
12. seed
13. heart
14. swell
15. enlighten
16. enlarge
17. nourish
18. fruit
19. neglect
20. word

Boggler #43—Scrambler #4

1. Aaron
2. Abinadi
3. Abish
4. Alma
5. Joseph
6. Jonas
7. Omner
8. Korihor
9. Teancum
10. Amlici
11. Laban
12. Kumen
13. Nephihah
14. Kishkumen
15. Moroni
16. Benjamin
17. Laman
18. Noah
19. Jacob
20. Mormon

Boggler #44—Scrambler #5

1. Ammaron
2. Shiz
3. Ammon
4. Lehi
5. Jared
6. Shiblon
7. Omni
8. Amalickiah
9. Lamoni

10. Jarom
11. Amaleki
12. Lemuel
13. Coriantor

14. Pahoran
15. Enos
16. Lib
17. Hagoth

18. Amlici
19. Sariah
20. Gideon

Boggler #45—Scrambler #6

1. Amos
2. Sam
3. Ishmael
4. Sherem
5. Shiz
6. Ether
7. Amulek

8. Mulek
9. Amaron
10. Kib
11. Chemish
12. Nephi
13. Gadianton
14. Noah

15. Ammoron
16. Mathoni
17. Limhi
18. Nehor
19. Samuel
20. Mosiah

Lesson Help Index #1

Youth Curriculum Topics

The Godhead
Bogglers #29 (part 4), #31, #34

The Plan of Salvation
Bogglers #12, #14, #19, #20, #21, #22, #29, #32

The Atonement of Jesus Christ
Bogglers #12, #19, #20, #22, #29, #41

The Apostasy and the Restoration
Bogglers #2, #7

Prophets and Revelation
Bogglers #3, #6, #8, #33

Priesthood and Priesthood Keys
Bogglers #8, #39

Ordinances and Covenants
Bogglers #13, #30, #40

Marriage and Family
Bogglers #9, #11, #37, #38

Commandments
Boggler #29 (parts 1–4)

Becoming More Christlike
Bogglers #17, #18, #29 (parts 1–2, 4–5)

Spiritual and Temporal Self-Reliance
Bogglers #18, #29 (parts 4–5)

Building the Kingdom of God
Boggler #2

Lesson Help Index #2

Elements of the Book of Mormon

About the Author

K evan J. Kennington was born in Star Valley, Wyoming, and raised on a small farm. Most of his adult life was spent teaching—as an LDS missionary, a seminary and institute teacher, and an award-winning public school administrator. He has also authored *Bible Brain Bogglers*. He has been married to his wife, Kathy Skapple Kennington, for forty years, and they are the parents of eight children and twenty-four grandchildren.